Breaking the Reading CODE

Phonics for Early Learners

A HANDBOOK FOR READING

by Mel A. Joseph

ISBN: 979-8-234-06934-4

Learning to read at an early age prepares children for academic success and establishes a strong foundation for a lifelong journey of learning.

To : ________________________________

From: ________________________________

Dedication

To my husband, Joe, who has dedicated a significant portion of his life to teaching young children and has been instrumental in bringing this book to life.

Special Thanks To :
E. A. Azana, Lyn Michael, and Brenda Natarajan
for your invaluable assistance in the creation of this book.

Note to the Parents

Breaking the Reading Code is a handbook designed to help parents teach their young children how to read.   It focuses on helping children learn how to "decode" words by breaking them into sounds. The process begins by first mastering the sounds of each letter and then blending the sounds to form sound blends. Finally, children will learn to combine the letter sounds and sound blends to form words. Once they have mastered this skill, they will be ready to read simple sentences and beginner-friendly books.

Some lessons in this handbook can be quite challenging for young learners, making consistent practice and repetition essential before advancing to a new lesson. Parents and teachers working with young children should limit their sessions to no more than 30 minutes each. Reading activities can be divided into two or three 30-minute sessions throughout the day. Once the children have developed the skills to decode words, they need to begin reading books. Start by providing them with easy-to-read texts that contain simple sentences, and gradually introduce more complex materials as their proficiency improves. With consistent practice, reading will soon become second nature.   For additional resources and other learning materials, please visit our website at www.jitpublishing.com.

About the Author

Mel Joseph has owned and operated learning centers in the United States for over ten years. Her extensive experience working individually with preschoolers in reading has inspired her to create this workbook. Its goal is to assist parents in teaching their young children how to read by utilizing a proven method detailed in this book. She firmly believes that children can develop reading skills at an early age, enabling them to read before entering first grade.

CONTENTS

CONTENTS

CONTENTS

ALPHABET SOUNDS

Aa  apple	**Bb**  bag	**Cc**  cup
Dd  dog	**Ee**  egg	**Ff**  frog
Gg  gift	**Hh**  hat	**Ii**  igloo
Jj  jam	**Kk**  kite	**Ll**  lion
Mm  map	**Nn**  nest	**Oo**  octopus
Pp  pot	**Qq**  queen	**Rr**  rocket
Ss  sun	**Tt**  turtle	**Uu**  umbrella
Vv  van	**Ww**  water	**Xx** 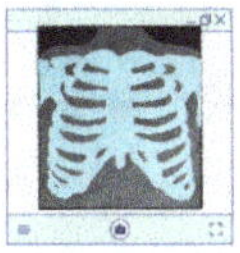 xray
Yy  yoyo	**Zz**  zebra	

LESSON 1 - SHORT VOWEL SOUNDS

a	**a**pple	**a**nt	**a**lligator
e	**e**gg	**e**lf	**e**lephant
i	**i**gloo	**i**tch	**i**nk
o	**o**x	**o**lives	**o**ctopus
u	 **u**mbrella	 **u**nder	 **u**pset

Note: Lessons on long vowel sounds start on page 114.

LESSON 1 - CONSONANT SOUNDS

Bb	 ball	 bat	 box
Cc	 car	 cat	 cup
Dd	 dad	 dog	 duck
Ff	 fan	 fish	 farm
Gg	 gift	 gum	 gate

CONSONANT SOUNDS

Hh	**h**at	**h**en	**h**op
Jj	**j**ar	**j**et	**j**ump
Kk	**k**iss	**k**ick	**k**ite
Ll	**l**amp	**l**og	**l**amb
Mm	**m**at	**m**om	**m**ilk

CONSONANT SOUNDS

Nn	 nap	 net	 nest
Pp	 pan	 pet	 puppy
Qq	 quack	 queen	 quail
Rr	 rat	 run	 rock
Ss	 sad	 sip	 soap

CONSONANT SOUNDS

Tt	**t**ag	**t**en	**t**ub
Vv	**v**an	**v**et	**v**est
Ww	**w**all	**w**ink	**w**agon
Xx	a**x**	bo**x**	fo**x**
Yy	**y**arn	**y**ellow	**y**oyo
Zz	**z**oo	**z**ip	**z**ebra

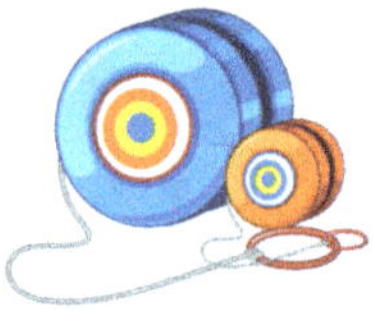

OTHER CONSONANT SOUNDS

Soft C, soft G and "z" sound of X

Cc (Soft)

circus　circle　celery

rice　dance　fence

Gg (Soft)

giant　giraffe　ginger

bridge　cage　stage

Xx (z sound)

xerox　xylophone

LESSON 2 – SHORT VOWEL AND CONSONANT BLENDS

*Say the short vowel and consonant sounds, then combine to form the sound blend. Ex. **a** and **d** for **ad**. Decode the word using the sound blend. Example: **d-ad** for the word **dad**.*

a → d → ad   dad 

a → g → ag   tag 

a → m → am   jam 

a → n → an   van 

a → p → ap   cap 

a → r → ar   jar 

a → t → at   cat 

LESSON 2 - SHORT VOWEL AND CONSONANT BLENDS

*Say the short vowel and consonant sounds, then combine to form the sound blend. Ex. **e** and **d** for **ed**. Decode the word using the sound blend. Example: **b-ed** for the word **bed.***

e → d → ed   bed 

e → g → eg   leg 

e → n → en   hen 

e → t → et   jet 

i → g → ig   dig 

i → n → in   bin 

i → p → ip   sip 

LESSON 2 - SHORT VOWEL AND CONSONANT BLENDS

Say the short vowel and consonant sounds, then combine to form the sound blend. Ex. o and g for og. Decode the word using the sound blend. Example: d-og for the word dog.

o → g → **og** **dog** 

o → p → **op** **pop** 

o → t → **ot** **hot** 

u → g → **ug** **bug** 

u → m → **um** **gum** 

u → n → **un** **sun** 

u → t → **ut** **nut** 

LESSON 2 – SHORT VOWEL AND CONSONANT BLENDS

*Say the **am** and **an** sound blends, then decode the words by breaking them into sounds. Example: **j-am** for **jam**.*

am

jam

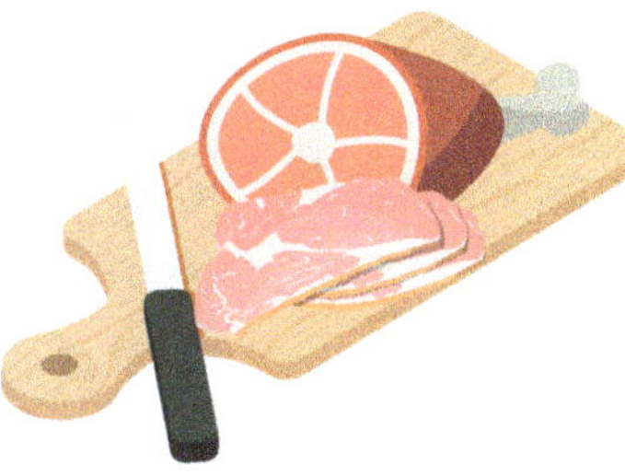

ham

ram

yam

an

can

fan

pan

van

Decode the words. Then, circle the correct word to match the picture on the right.

yam   ram 

can   fan 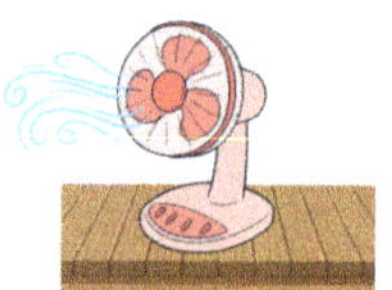

ram   ham 

yam   jam 

fan   pan 

can   man 

ram   ham 

van   tan 

LESSON 2 - SHORT VOWEL AND CONSONANT BLENDS

*Say the **ad** and **ag** sound blends, then decode the words by breaking them into sounds. Example: **d-ad** for **dad**.*

ad

dad

mad

pad

sad

ag

bag

rag

tag

wag

Decode the words. Then, circle the correct word to match the picture on the right.

mad	**pad**	
sad	**dad**	
wag	**tag**	
pad	**sad**	
bag	**rag**	
dad	**pad**	
sag	**tag**	
rag	**bag**	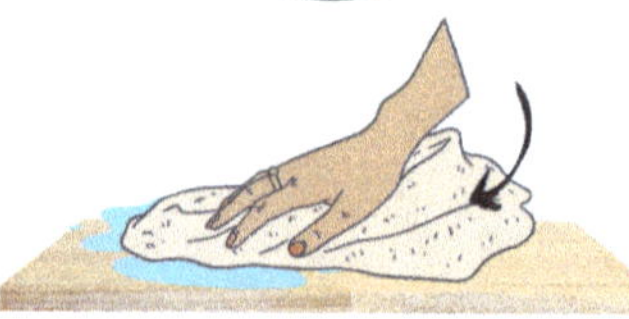

LESSON 2 – SHORT VOWEL AND CONSONANT BLENDS

*Say the **ap**, **ar**, and **at** sound blends, then decode the words by breaking them into sounds. Example: **m-ap** for **map**.*

ap

map **cap**

tap **nap**

ar

bar **car**

jar **far**

at

bat **cat**

hat **mat**

LESSON 2 – SHORT VOWEL AND CONSONANT BLENDS

Decode the words. Then, circle the correct word to match the picture on the right.

tap   **n**ap

cat   **m**at

hat   **r**at

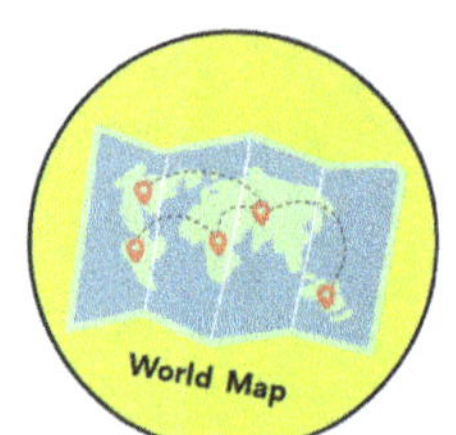

nap   **m**ap

bar   **c**ar

jar   **f**ar

hat   **b**at

fat   **m**at

LESSON 2 - SHORT VOWEL AND CONSONANT BLENDS

*Say the ed and eg sound blends, then decode the words by breaking them into sounds. Example: **b-ed** for **bed**.*

ed

bed

red

fed

wed

eg

beg

leg

peg

keg

LESSON 2 - SHORT VOWEL AND CONSONANT BLENDS

Decode the words. Then, circle the correct word to match the picture on the right.

beg	**leg**	
red	**bed**	
fed	**wed**	
leg	**keg**	
beg	**peg**	
wed	**fed**	
red	**bed**	

LESSON 2 - SHORT VOWEL AND CONSONANT BLENDS

*Say the en and et sound blends, then decode the words by breaking them into sounds. Example: **d-en** for **den**.*

en

den

hen

pen

men

et

jet

pet

vet

wet

LESSON 2 – SHORT VOWEL AND CONSONANT BLENDS

Decode the words. Then, circle the correct word to match the picture on the right.

men	**p**en

den	**h**en

jet	**v**et

wet	**g**et

ten	**m**en

hen	**p**en

vet	**j**et

pet	**w**et

*Say the ig, in, and ip sound blends, then decode the words by breaking them into sounds. Example: **b-ig** for **big**.*

LESSON 2 – SHORT VOWEL AND CONSONANT BLENDS

Decode the words. Then, circle the correct word to match the picture on the right.

big   fig

fin   bin

pin   win

fig   big

bin   fin

pin   tin

dip   tip

lip   sip

LESSON 2 - SHORT VOWEL AND CONSONANT BLENDS

*Say the **og**, **op**, and **ot** sound blends, then decode the words by breaking them into sounds. Example: **d-og** for **dog**.*

LESSON 2 – SHORT VOWEL AND CONSONANT BLENDS

Decode the words. Then, circle the correct word to match the picture on the right.

hot   pot 

log   fog 

hog   dog 

pop   top 

mop   hop 

rot   hot 

top   mop 

pop   hop 

LESSON 2 – SHORT VOWEL AND CONSONANT BLENDS

*Say the **ub** and **ug** sound blends, then decode the words by breaking them into sounds. Example: **c-ub** for **cub**.*

ub

cub

rub

tub

ug

bug

mug

hug

tug

tug   **m**ug

hug   **b**ug

tub   **r**ub

pub   **c**ub

tug   **d**ug

cub   **r**ub

pug   **h**ug

LESSON 2 – SHORT VOWEL AND CONSONANT BLENDS

Say the **un** *and* **ut** *sound blends, then decode the words by breaking them into sounds. Example:* **b-un** *for* **bun**.

bun

fun

sun

run

cut

hut

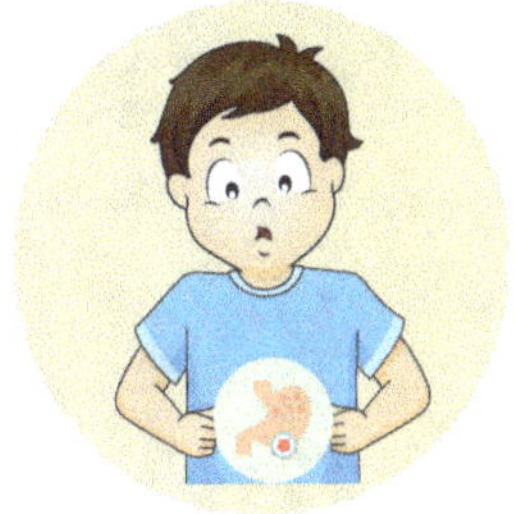

nut

gut

Decode the words. Then, circle the correct word to match the picture on the right.

run	bun	
fun	sun	
nut	hut	
bun	run	
hut	cut	
run	sun	
nut	cut	

27

LESSON 2 – SHORT VOWEL AND CONSONANT BLENDS

Read the phrases, then draw a line to match the picture on the right.

a jar of **jam**

ram by the barn

a hot **pan**

can of **ham**

cat in a pot

bat on top

ants in a **jar**

dog in a **car**

Read the phrases, then draw a line to match the picture on the right.

a red **bin**

a big **win**

a dark **den**

a fat **hen**

a **wet** mop

a fast **jet**

frog on a **log**

hog in the mud

Read the phrases, then draw a line to match the picture on the right.

dot on a cup

hop on a mat

a big **pop**

a hot **pot**

toys in a **tub**

a big **hug**

tag on a **rug**

a **cub** by its dad

SHORT VOWEL AND CONSONANT BLENDS REVIEW

ad
dad
mad
pad
sad

ag
bag
tag
rag
wag

am
jam
ham
ram
yam

an
can
fan
man
van

ap
cap
map
nap
tap

ar
bar
car
far
jar

at
bat
cat
hat
mat

ed
bed
fed
red
wed

eg
beg
keg
leg
peg

en
den
hen
men
ten

et
jet
pet
met
wet

SHORT VOWEL AND
CONSONANT BLEND REVIEW

ig

big
dig
fig
wig

in

bin
fin
tin
win

ip

dip
rip
tip
sip

og

dog
fog
hog
log

op

hop
mop
pop
top

ot

dot
hot
pot
rot

ug

bug
hug
mug
tug

um

hum
gum
sum
yum

un

bun
fun
run
sun

ut

cut
nut
gut
hut

LESSON 3 - CONSONANT CLUSTERS (L-BLENDS)

*Sound out each letter, then combine the sounds of the letter blends. Ex. **b** and **l** for **bl,** **c** and **l** for **cl***

LESSON 3 - CONSONANT CLUSTERS (L-BLENDS)

*Say the sound of **bl** and **cl** blends, then read the whole word. (Do not decode words at this point).*

bl

block

blue

blow

blast

cl

clap

clock

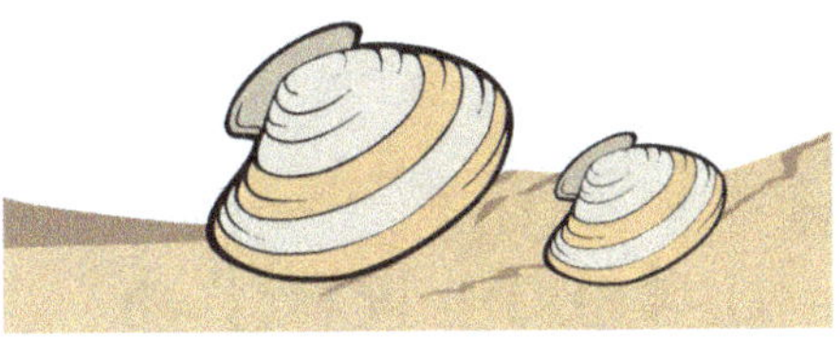

clam

clown

LESSON 3 - CONSONANT CLUSTERS (L-BLENDS)

*Read the words with **bl** and **cl** sound blends, then circle the word that matches the picture. Use the sentence as a hint.*

blink

blank

blend

blue

black

bloom

A _______ bird sits on the window pane.

clip

clean

class

cling

clap

clamp

The __________ listens to the teacher.

LESSON 3 - CONSONANT CLUSTERS (L-BLENDS)

*Say the sound of **fl** and **gl** blends, then read the whole word. (Do not decode words at this point).*

fl

flag

flask

flock

float

gl

glass

globe

glue

glide

LESSON 3 - CONSONANT CLUSTERS (L-BLENDS)

*Read the words with **fl** and **gl** sound blends, then circle the word that matches the picture. Use the sentence as a hint.*

flat      **fl**ips

flow   **fl**ame

flop   **fl**oor

The cook __________ the pancake off the pan.

glad      **gl**ee

glow   **gl**oss

gloves   **gl**and

Mom wear __________ in the garden.

LESSON 3 - CONSONANT CLUSTERS (L-BLENDS)

*Say the sound of **pl** and **sl** blends, then read the whole word. (Do not decode words at this point).*

pl

plum

plant

play

plate

sl

sled

slip

sleep

slide

*Read the words with **pl** and **sl** sound blends, then circle the word that matches the picture. Use the sentence as a hint.*

plan   **pl**ot

plug   **pl**um

pluck   **pl**ane

The _________ flies above the cloud.

slap   **sl**ing

slam   **sl**ug

slow   **sl**oth

The _________ clings on the tree branch.

Read the words. Then, complete the sentence using the pictures as hints.

| **blocks** | **blow** | **bloom** |

I ___________ the candles on the cake.

The girls stack the ___________.

The flowers ___________ in the garden.

| **climb** | **clown** | **cloud** |

The ___________ juggles the balls.

The boys ___________ the steep rock.

The sun hides behind the dark ___________.

Read the words. Then, complete the sentence using the pictures as hints.

flock   flag   floor

The winner holds a _______ in his hand.

A _______ of birds fly above the trees.

The baby loves to sleep on the _______.

glass   glide   glue

The kites _______ in the sky.

The _______ is very sticky.

The fish tank is made of clear _______.

Read the words. Then, complete the sentence using the pictures as hints.

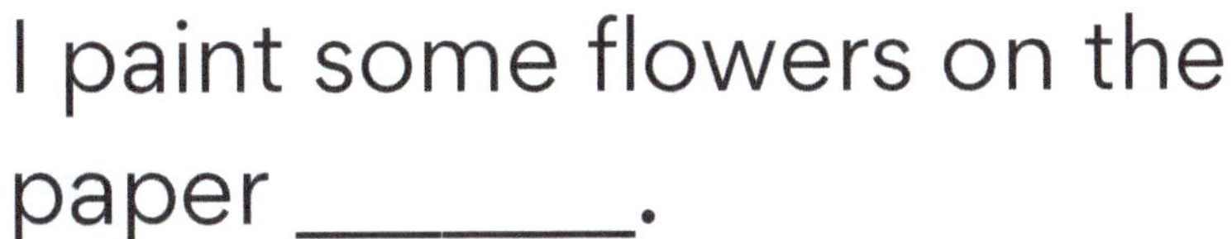

plate   play   plums

We love to __________ in the rain.

I paint some flowers on the paper _______.

The _______ are sweet and juicy.

slow   sleep   slide

Jane and her cat _________ by the window.

It is fun to play on the __________.

The _________ turtle won the race.

CONSONANT CLUSTERS (L-BLENDS)

Practice the sound combinations then read the whole word.

bl	**bl**ock	**bl**ue	**bl**ow
cl	**cl**ap	**cl**ock	**cl**am
fl	**fl**ag	**fl**ask	**fl**y
gl	**gl**ass	**gl**oves	**gl**ue
pl	**pl**um	**pl**ant	**pl**ay
sl	**sl**ed	**sl**am	**sl**ug

LESSON 4 - CONSONANT CLUSTERS (R-BLENDS)

Sound out each letter, then combine the sounds of the letter blends. Ex. **b** *and* **r** *for* **br**, **c** *and* **r** *for* **cr** *etc.*

LESSON 4 – CONSONANT CLUSTERS (R-BLENDS)

*Say the sound of **br** and **cr** blends, then read the whole word. (Do not decode words at this point).*

br

bread

bricks

broom

brush

cr

crab

crib

crack

crown

LESSON 4 – CONSONANT CLUSTERS (R-BLENDS)

*Read the words with **br** and **cr** sound blends, then circle the word that matches the picture.   Use the sentence as a hint.*

brag   **brisk**

bread   **brave**

braid   **brain**

Tara's long _________ looks pretty.

crop   **craft**

creek   **crawls**

crown   **crumb**

The baby __________ under the table.

LESSON 4 - CONSONANT CLUSTERS (R-BLENDS)

Say the sound of dr and fr blends, then read the whole word. (Do not decode words at this point).

dr

draw

dress

drink

drum

fr

frog

fruit

friend

front

LESSON 4 - CONSONANT CLUSTERS (R-BLENDS)

*Read the words with the **dr** and **fr** sound blends, then circle the word that matches the picture. Use the sentence as a hint.*

drop **dr**ink

draw **dr**ift

drum **dr**eam

The dogs __________ of playing in the park.

frog **fr**ee

front **fr**esh

frown **fr**ame

The bird wants to be ________.

LESSON 4 – CONSONANT CLUSTERS (R-BLENDS)

Say the sound of gr and pr blends, then read the whole word. (Do not decode words at this point).

gr

grass

gray

grapes

grill

pr

pray

prune

prince

print

LESSON 4 - CONSONANT CLUSTERS (R-BLENDS)

*Read the words with **gr** and **pr** sound blends, then circle the word that matches the picture. Use the sentence as a hint.*

grip　　**grab**

gray　　**green**

grill　　**grow**

The plants __________ in the garden.

prey　　**print**

press　　**proud**

prize　　**prick**

I __________ the button to ring the doorbell.

LESSON 4 – CONSONANT CLUSTERS (R-BLENDS)

*Say the sound of **tr** blend, then read the whole word. (Do not decode words at this point).*

tree

train

truck

trout

---

*Read the words with the **tr** sound blend, then circle the word that matches the picture. Use the sentence asa hint .*

trip

trap

trick

trim

trunk

treats

The basket is full of sweet _______.

LESSON 4

Read the words, then complete the sentence using the pictures as hints.

| **brush** | **brown** | **bricks** |

The __________ bear sleeps in a cave.

Kayla paints flowers with a ____________.

The men stack the ________.

| **crack** | **crunchy** | **crab** |

The _______ crawls on the sand.

Fresh apples are sweet and __________ .

The chicks ___________ the eggshells.

LESSON 4

Read the words, then complete the sentence using the pictures as hints.

| **friend** | **frog** | **fruits** |

The ________ waits for its prey.

I love to eat fresh ________.

Mark walks to school with his ________ Nate.

| **draw** | **dress** | **drums** |

I play ________ at the school fair.

Jen loves to ________ the sky.

The girl dreams of a red ________.

Read the words, then complete the sentence using the pictures as hints.

---

grill   green   growl

The lion made an angry

___________.

Dad cooks a fish on the

___________.

My ___________ jacket keeps
me dry.

---

pretty   prince   pray

The ___________ lives in a
huge castle.

I ___________ before I go to
bed.

The girl looks ___________ in
a blue dress.

CONSONANT CLUSTERS (R-BLENDS)

Practice the sound combinations then read the whole word.

br	**br**own	**br**ush	**br**oom
cr	**cr**ab	**cr**ib	**cr**ack
dr	**dr**aw	**dr**ess	**dr**um
fr	**fr**og	**fr**uit	**fr**iend
gr	**gr**ass	**gr**een	**gr**apes
pr	**pr**ay	**pr**esent	**pr**ince
tr	**tr**ee	**tr**ain	**tr**uck

LESSON 5 - CONSONANT CLUSTERS (S-BLENDS)

Sound out each letter, then combine the sounds of the letter blends. Ex. **s and c** *for* **sc**, **s and m** *for* **sm**, *etc*

LESSON 5 - CONSONANT CLUSTERS (S-BLENDS)

*Say the sound of sc and sk blends, then read the whole word.
(Do not decode words at this point).*

sc

scarf

scalp

score

scale

sk

ski

skirt

skunk

skates

LESSON 5 - CONSONANT CLUSTERS (S-BLENDS)

*Read the words with **sc** and **sk** sound blends, then circle the word that matches the picture. Use the sentence as a hint.*

scar

scan

scold

scare

scale

scout

The girl ___________ stands to honor the flag.

skin

skid

skip

skim

skunk

skull

Kayla loves to play ________ rope with her sister.

LESSON 5 – CONSONANT CLUSTERS (S-BLENDS)

*Say the sound of **sm** and **sn** blends, then read the whole word. (Do not decode words at this point).*

sm

smell

smile

smoke

smart

sn

snow

snake

snack

sniff

*Read the words with **sm** and **sn** sound blends, then circle the word that matches the picture. Use the sentence as a hint.*

smog

small

smart

smash

smear

smile

The _________ boy scored high on his test.

snap

snag

snort

sniff

snail

snug

The hungry _________ ate the leaves.

LESSON 5 - CONSONANT CLUSTERS (S-BLENDS)

Say the sound of sp and st blends, then read the whole word.
(Do not decode words at this point).

sp

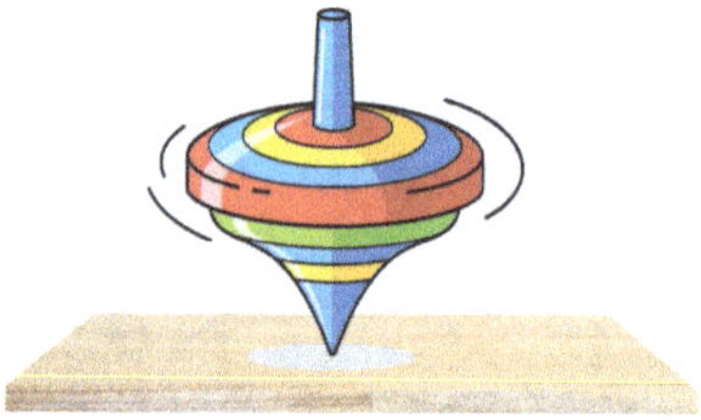

spin

spark

spill

sponge

st

star

stop

stack

stairs

LESSON 5 - CONSONANT CLUSTERS (S-BLENDS)

*Read the words with **sp** and **st** sound blends, then circle the word that matches the picture. Use the sentence as a hint.*

spell　　　**spot**

spoon　　　**spark**

speed　　　**speak**

Mark will ___________ at the party.

star　　　**stem**

step　　　**stop**

start　　　**stamp**

I ___________ on the ladder to reach the fruit.

LESSON 5 – CONSONANT CLUSTERS (S-BLENDS)

Say the sound of **sw** *blends, then read the whole word.*
(Do not decode words at this point.)

sw

swim

sweep

swing

sweat

Read the words with the **sw** *sound blend, then circle the word that matches the picture. Use the sentence as a hint.*

swap

swell

swan

swim

sweet

swift

The white _________ swims in the lake.

Read the words. Then, complete the sentence using the correct word.   Use the pictures as hints.

scarf	scare	score

My thick __________ keeps my neck warm.

Ben got a high __________ on his test.

The bees __________ the boy.

ski	skunk	skirt

The __________ lives under a pile of leaves.

It is fun to ______ in the winter.

I dance in my pink __________.

LESSON 5

Read the words. Then, complete the sentence using the correct word.   Use the pictures as hints.

small   **smile**   **smell**

I love to ___________ flowers in the garden.

The proud winner gave a big ___________.

The baby chases the ___________ puppy.

snake   **snow**   **sniff**

The ___________ falls on the mountain.

The dog likes to ___________ shoes.

The ___________ hides behind the bushes.

Read the words. Then, complete the sentence using the correct word.   Use the pictures as hints.

---

spin   spot   spark

The sea lion has a black __________ on its chest.

We will ________ the wheel to win the prize.

The ________ lights up the sky.

---

stops   sticks   stack

We _________ the books on the table.

The blue car ________ at the red light.

The beaver builds a house made of _________.

LESSON 5

Read the words. Then, complete the sentence using the correct word.   Use the pictures as hints.

slam   sled   slope

The rocks rolled on a steep ________.

The player will ________ the ball in the hoop.

My ________ moves fast on an icy slope.

sweeps   swing   swim

The ducks ________ under the bridge.

Jen ________ the dirt on the floor.

The girl loves to ________ on the tree branch.

CONSONANT CLUSTERS (S-BLENDS)

Practice the sound combinations then read the whole word.

sc	**sc**arf	**sc**alp	**sc**ore
sk	**sk**i	**sk**irt	**sk**unk
sl	**sl**eep	**sl**ing	**sl**oth
sm	**sm**ell	**sm**art	**sm**oke
sn	**sn**ow	**sn**ake	**sn**ack
sp	**sp**in	**sp**ark	**sp**ill
st	**st**ar	**st**ack	**st**ep
sw	**sw**im	**sw**eep	**sw**ing

LESSON 6 - OTHER CONSONANT CLUSTERS

Sound out each sound blend, then combine them together.
***Ex. sc/r** for **scr**, **sq/u** for **squ**, **st/r** for **str**, **th/r** for **thr**, **sp/r** for **spr**, **sp/l** for spl.*

LESSON 6 – OTHER CONSONANT CLUSTERS

Say the sound of scr and squ blends, then read the whole word. (Do not decode words at this point).

scr

scratch

screw

scrub

screen

squ

square

squash

squirrel

squid

LESSON 6 - OTHER CONSONANT CLUSTERS

Circle the word that matches the picture. Then, complete the sentence with the correct word.

scrap

scrubs

scroll

screw

Mom _______ the dirt with a brush.

squash

squint

squirt

squeak

I can hear a loud _______ when I open the door.

LESSON 6 – OTHER CONSONANT CLUSTERS

Say the sound of str and spr blends, then read the whole word. (Do not decode words at this point).

straw

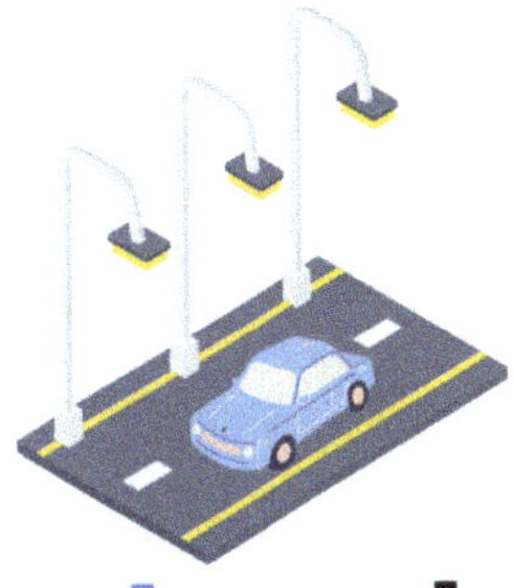

street

stripe

strong

spring

spray

spread

sprout

LESSON 6 - OTHER CONSONANT CLUSTERS

Circle the word that matches the picture. Then, complete the sentence with the correct word.

strap

strip

strand

stream

The ________ runs near the red barn.

sprig

spray

sprint

spread

I ________ jelly on my toast.

LESSON 6 – OTHER CONSONANT CLUSTERS

Say the sound of spl, thr, and tw sound blends, then read the whole word. (Do not decode words at this point).

spl

splash

split

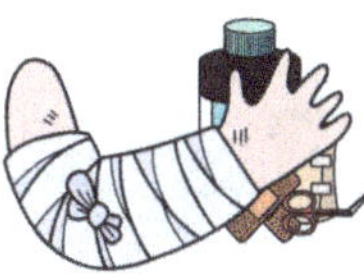

splint

splice

thr

throw

thread

three

throat

tw

twin

twig

twirl

twist

LESSON 6 - OTHER CONSONANT CLUSTERS

Circle the word that matches the picture. Then, complete the sentence with the correct word.

splice

split

splash

splint

I made a big _________ in the pool.

throw

throne

thrill

throb

The king sits on his _________.

twirl

twist

twelve

twinkle

The stars _________ in the night sky.

OTHER CONSONANT CLUSTERS

Practice the sound combinations then read the whole word.

scr	scratch	screw	scrub
squ	square	squash	squirrel
str	straw	street	strong
spr	spring	spray	spread
spl	splash	split	splint
thr	throw	thread	throat
tw	twin	twist	twirl

LESSON 7 - ENDING CONSONANT CLUSTERS

*Sound out each letter, then combine the sounds of the letter blends. Ex. **c** and **t** for **ct**, **l** and **d** for **ld**.*

LESSON 7 - ENDING CONSONANT CLUSTERS

Say the sound of ct and ft blends, then read the whole word.
(Do not decode words at this point).

act

pact

select

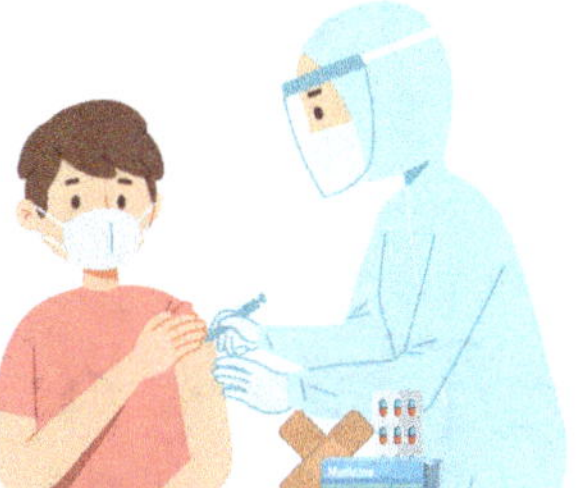

inject

gift

lift

raft

soft

LESSON 7 - ENDING CONSONANT CLUSTERS

Circle the word that matches the picture. Then, complete the sentence with the correct word.

act   **pa**ct

erect   **eje**ct

The children _______ on the stage.

soft   **si**ft

drift   **shi**ft

I help my grandma ________ the flour.

LESSON 7 – ENDING CONSONANT CLUSTERS

*Say the sound of **ld** and **lp** blends, then read the whole word. (Do not decode words at this point).*

bald

cold

fold

gold

help

scalp

pulp

gulp

LESSON 7 - ENDING CONSONANT CLUSTERS

Circle the word that matches the picture. Then, complete the sentence with the correct word.

bald   **cold**

hold   **fold**

I help my mom _______ my clothes.

kelp   **help**

gulp   **pulp**

I _______ my brother clean up the yard.

LESSON 7 - ENDING CONSONANT CLUSTERS

*Say the sound of **lt** and **mp** blends, then read the whole word. (Do not decode words at this point).*

belt

melt

salt

tilt

ramp

jump

camp

lamp

LESSON 7 - ENDING CONSONANT CLUSTERS

Circle the word that matches the picture. Then, complete the sentence with the correct word.

melt   **be**lt

halt   **bo**lt

I put a black ___________ on the snowman.

jump   **pu**mp

stamp   **da**mp

Dad will ___________ air into my bike's tire.

LESSON 7 - ENDING CONSONANT CLUSTERS

Say the sound of nd and nk blends, then read the whole word. (Do not decode words at this point).

nd

sand

band

bend

friend

nk

pink

bunk

wink

think

LESSON 7 - ENDING CONSONANT CLUSTERS

Circle the word that matches the picture. Then, complete the sentence with the correct word.

wand   pond

bland   sand

The duck waits for its ducklings to cross the __________.

tank   bank

chunk   blank

The bottle sank to the bottom of the fish __________.

ENDING CONSONANT CLUSTERS

Practice the sound combinations then read the whole word.

ct	act	pact	inject
ft	gift	left	soft
ld	cold	fold	gold
lp	help	gulp	pulp
lt	belt	melt	salt
mp	ramp	jump	camp
nd	sand	wand	bend
nk	pink	wink	tank

LESSON 7 - ENDING CONSONANT CLUSTERS

Sound out each letter, then combine the sounds of the letter blends. Ex. **n** *and* **t** *for* **nt**, **r** *and* **d** *for* **rd**

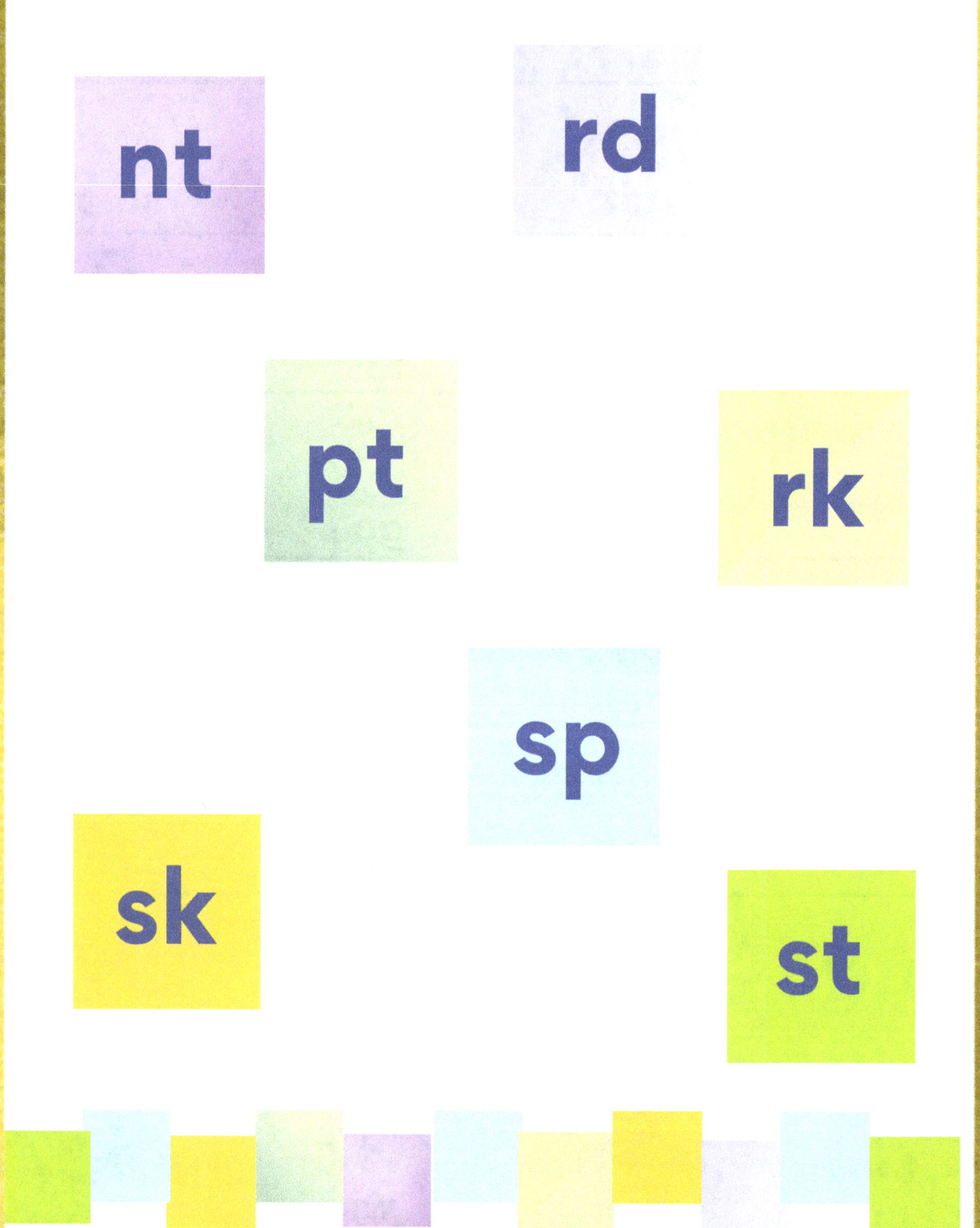

*Say the sound of **nt** and **pt** blends, then read the whole word. (Do not decode words at this point).*

nt

dent

tent

plant

paint

pt

slept

wept

erupt

sculpt

Circle the word that matches the picture. Then, complete the sentence with the correct word.

plant      **slant**

count   **mount**

The boys __________ the coins from the piggy bank.

crept      **swept**

sculpt   **script**

I __________ a dolphin from a block of ice.

LESSON 7 - ENDING CONSONANT CLUSTERS

*Say the sound of **rd** and **rk** blends, then read the whole word. (Do not decode words at this point).*

rd

bird

card

yard

board

rk

park

bark

shark

dark

LESSON 7 – ENDING CONSONANT CLUSTERS

Circle the word that matches the picture. Then, complete the sentence with the correct word.

cord

sword

beard

third

Sam won __________ place at a school contest.

fork

work

bark

spark

The dogs ________ at the owl in the park.

LESSON 7 - ENDING CONSONANT CLUSTERS

*Say the sound of **sk, sp,** and **st** blends, then read the whole word. (Do not decode words at this point).*

sk

mask

disk

desk

whisk

sp

crisp

wasp

clasp

grasp

st

twist

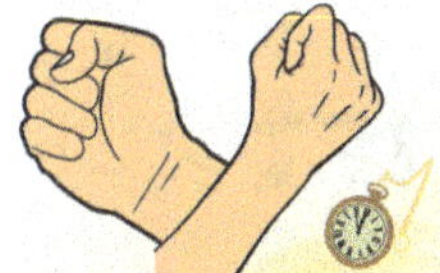

fist

rest

chest

LESSON 7 – ENDING CONSONANT CLUSTERS

Circle the word that matches the picture. Then, complete the sentence with the correct word.

task   **fla**sk

wisk   **bri**sk

The plant grows inside the __________.

gasp   **gra**sp

wasp   **cri**sp

The __________ builds its nest in the tree.

fist   **mi**st

toast   **roa**st

Mom served __________ chicken for lunch.

ENDING CONSONANT CLUSTERS

Practice the sound combinations then read the whole word.

nt	de**nt**	pla**nt**	pai**nt**
pt	sle**pt**	we**pt**	eru**pt**
rd	bi**rd**	ca**rd**	ya**rd**
rk	pa**rk**	ba**rk**	sha**rk**
sk	ma**sk**	de**sk**	whi**sk**
sp	cri**sp**	wa**sp**	cla**sp**
st	twi**st**	che**st**	toa**st**

LESSON 8 - CONSONANT DIGRAPH

Say the sound of each sound blend.

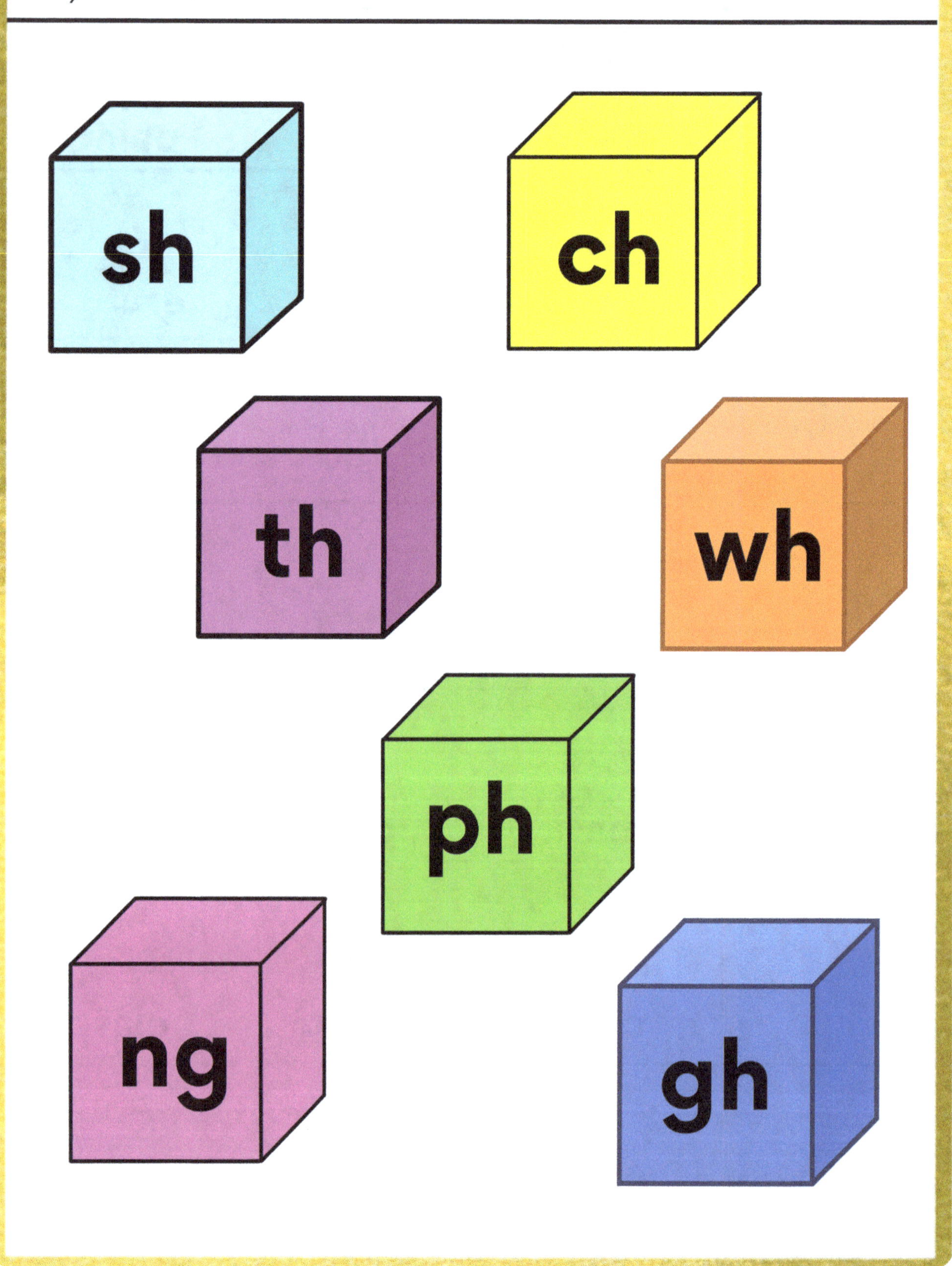

LESSON 8 - CONSONANT DIGRAPH

Say the sound of sh blend, then read the whole word. Pay attention to the position of the sound blends.

(Beginning sound)

shirt

ship

shell

shoes

(Ending sound)

mash

fish

push

trash

LESSON 8 - CONSONANT DIGRAPH

Circle the word that matches the picture. Then, complete the sentence with the correct word.

(Beginning sound)

shirt

shell

ship

shop

The ___________ sails towards the east.

(Ending sound)

fish

mash

push

trash

The garbage bin is full of dirty ______________.

LESSON 8 - CONSONANT DIGRAPH

Say the sound of ch blend, then read the whole word. Pay attention to the position of the sound blends.

ch (Beginning sound)

cheese

chalk

cherry

church

ch (Ending sound)

bench

lunch

catch

match

LESSON 8 - CONSONANT DIGRAPH

Circle the word that matches the picture. Then, complete the sentence with the correct word.

(Beginning sound)

chalk

cheese

cherry

church

The mouse ate a block of ___________.

(Ending sound)

ca**tch**

ma**tch**

lu**nch**

pu**nch**

I packed my school ___________.

LESSON 8 - CONSONANT DIGRAPH

Say the sound of th blend, then read the whole word. Pay attention to the position of the sound blends.

th

(Beginning sound)

think

thick

three

thumb

th

(Ending sound)

bath

math

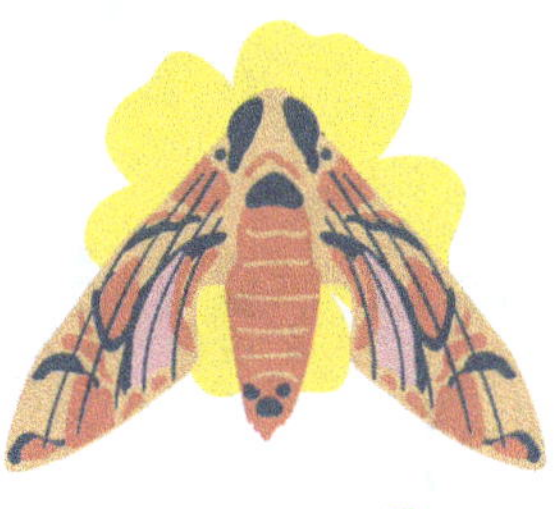

moth

sloth

LESSON 8 – CONSONANT DIGRAPH

Circle the word that matches the picture. Then, complete the sentence with the correct word.

(Beginning sound)

thick

think

three

thumb

Dan hides behind the
__________ bushes.

(Ending sound)

path

bath

moth

sloth

Bubba loves to take a
bubble __________.

LESSON 8 - CONSONANT DIGRAPH

Say the sound of th and wh blend, then read the whole word.
Pay attention to the position of the sound blends.

th

(Beginning sound)

this

that

there

they

wh

(Beginning sound)

whale

wheel

whisk

whisper

LESSON 8 - CONSONANT DIGRAPH

Circle the word that matches the picture. Then, complete the sentence with the correct word.

(Beginning sound)

that

this

there

They

Jake and Jen are friends. _________ love to dance.

(Beginning sound)

when

white

whisk

whale

A blue _________ jumps out of the water.

LESSON 8 - CONSONANT DIGRAPH

Say the sound of ph, ng, and gh blends, then read the whole word. Pay attention to the position of the sound blends.

ph
(Beginning sound)

phone

photo

pharaoh

ng
(Ending sound)

si**ng**

wi**ng**

sli**ng**

gh
(Ending sound)

lau**gh**

cou**gh**

rou**gh**

LESSON 8 - CONSONANT DIGRAPH

Circle the word that matches the picture. Then, complete the sentence using the correct word.

(Beginning sound)

phone

photo

pharaoh

We hang the _________ on the wall.

(Ending sound)

si**ng**

wi**ng**

sli**ng**

I help my sister put on the _________.

(Ending sound)

cou**gh**

lau**gh**

rou**gh**

We _______ at the funny joke.

CONSONANT DIGRAPHS

Practice the sound combinations then read the whole word.

sh Beginning sound	 **sh**irt	 **sh**ark	 **sh**ell
sh Ending sound	 ma**sh**	 fi**sh**	 bru**sh**
ch Beginning sound	 **ch**eese	 **ch**alk	 **ch**erry
ch Ending sound	 ben**ch**	 lun**ch**	 chur**ch**
th Beginning sound (Soft "th" Sound)	 **th**umb	 **th**ick	 **th**ink
th Ending sound (Soft "th" Sound)	 ba**th**	 slo**th**	 ma**th**

CONSONANT DIGRAPHS

Practice the sound combinations then read the whole word.

th
Beginning sound
(Hard "th" Sound)

this **that** **there**

wh
Beginning sound

whale **wheel** **whisk**

ph
Beginning sound

phone **photo** **pharaoh**

ng
Ending sound

ring **sing** **wing**

gh
Ending sound

laugh **cough** **rough**

LESSON 9 - DOUBLE CONSONANTS

Practice the sound combinations then read the whole word.

ss	class	grass	dress
ll	bell	doll	drill
tt	butter	bitter	letter
tt	kitten	mittens	rotten
ff	cliff	muff	fluff
bb	rabbit	bubble	pebble

LESSON 9 - DOUBLE CONSONANTS

Practice the sound combinations then read the whole word.

dd	 **fiddle**	 **ladder**	 **muddy**
pp	 **puppy**	 **happy**	 **pepper**
gg	 **goggle**	 **juggle**	 **buggy**
mm	 **hammer**	 **drummer**	 **swimmer**
rr	 **berry**	 **carry**	 **cherry**
zz	 **fuzzy**	 **dizzy**	 **puzzle**

LESSON 9 - DOUBLE CONSONANTS

Circle the word that matches the picture. Then, complete the sentence with the correct word.

bless

press

guess

Can you _________ what is in the box?

chilly

pillow

yellow

I love to hug soft and fluffy _________.

better

critter

glitter

The stars _________ in the night sky.

LESSON 9 - DOUBLE CONSONANTS

Circle the word that matches the picture. Then, complete the sentence using the correct word.

bitten

mitten

cotton

My _________ candy is soft and fluffy.

coffee

fluffy

puffy

The boy wears a _______ jacket.

bubble

chubby

rubble

The _________ cat likes to take a nap.

LESSON 9 – DOUBLE CONSONANTS

Circle the word that matches the picture. Then, complete the sentence with the correct word.

hidd**en**

midd**le**

ladd**er**

Eggs are _________ under the bushes.

happ**y**

pupp**y**

pepp**er**

The _________ puppy wags its tail.

wigg**le**

jugg**le**

gigg**le**

The clown loves to _________ the rings.

LESSON 9 - DOUBLE CONSONANTS

Circle the word that matches the picture. Then, complete the sentence with the correct word.

simm**er**

summ**er**

yumm**y**

We love to visit the farm in the __________.

ferr**y**

furr**y**

flurr**y**

I love to cuddle soft and __________ animals.

dazz**le**

puzz**le**

buzz**er**

Press the __________ to open the door.

LESSON 10 – LONG VOWEL SOUNDS

a	 acorn	 apron	 ape
e	 eel	 eat	 eagle
i	 ice	 island	 ivy
o	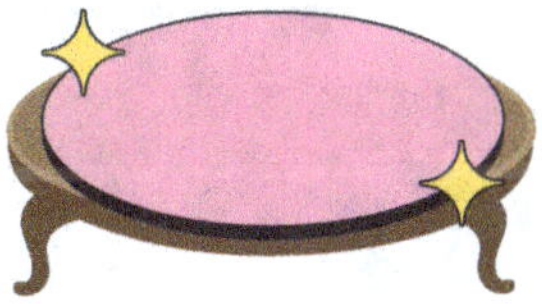 oval	 old	 orange
u	 unicorn ("yoo" sound)	 ukulele ("yoo" sound)	 ruler ("oo" sound)

LESSON 10 - COMPARING SHORT AND LONG VOWEL SOUNDS

Short Vowel Sound	Long Vowel Sound
a **a**pple	a **acorn**
e **e**gg	e **eel**
i **i**gloo	i **ice**
o **o**ctopus	o **orange**
u **umbrella**	u **unicorn** "yoo" sound **ruler** "oo" sound

LESSON 10 - VOWEL DIGRAPHS /DIPHTHONGS

ai long a sound	 rain	 chair	 paint
ea long e sound	 eat	 meat	 treat
ea short e sound	 head	 bread	 thread
ea long a sound	 bear	 pear	 tear
ee long e sound	 beet	 sweet	 street
ey long e sound	 monkey	 donkey	 honey

LESSON 10 - VOWEL DIGRAPHS /DIPHTHONGS

oa long o sound	 **boat**	 **goat**	 **float**
ow long o sound	 **blow**	 **grow**	 **snow**
oy "oi" sound	 **boy**	 **joy**	 **toy**
au short o sound	 **haul**	 **haunt**	 **vault**
aw short o sound	 **claw**	 **fawn**	 **hawk**

LESSON 10 – VOWEL DIGRAPHS /DIPHTHONGS

ei long a sound	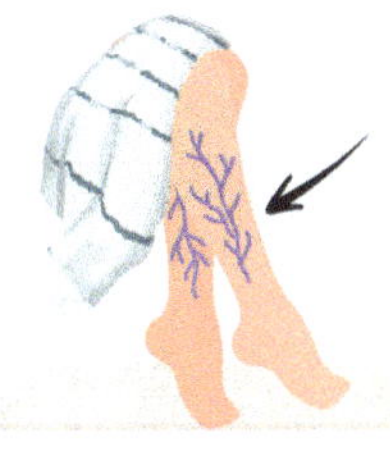 **vein**	 **veil**	 **weigh**
ie long e sound	 **field**	 **piece**	 **movie**
ay long a sound	 **play**	 **pray**	 **spray**
ui long u sound ("oo")	 **suit**	 **fruit**	 **juice**
ui short i sound	 **build**	 **guilt**	 **guitar**

LESSON 10 - VOWEL DIGRAPHS /DIPHTHONGS

oe long o sound	 **doe**	 **toe**	 **hoe**
ue long u sound "oo"	 **clue**	 **blue**	 **glue**
ew long u sound "yoo"	 **dew**	 **new**	 **stew**
oo long sound	 **moon**	 **goose**	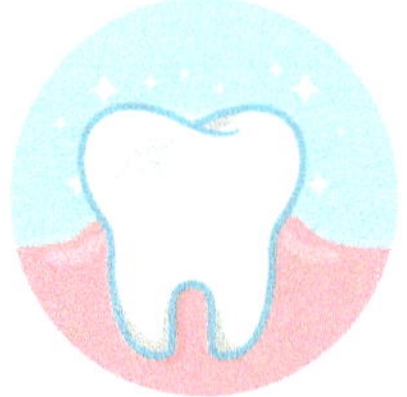 **tooth**
oo short sound	 **book**	 **cook**	 **look**

LESSON 10 – VOWEL DIGRAPHS /DIPHTHONGS

oi "oy" sound	 **oil**	 **coin**	 **boil**
ou "ow" sound	 **cloud**	 **flour**	 **house**
ou long o sound	 **tour**	 **pour**	 **four**
ou "uh" sound	 **cough**	 **touch**	 **double**
ou long u sound "oͦo"	 **group**	 **soup**	 **gourd**

LESSON 10 - SHORT AND LONG VOWEL SOUND CONTRAST

Silent "e" : Observe how the short vowel sound changes to long vowel sound when "e" was added at the end of the word. The "e" at the end become silent.

Short Vowel	Long Vowel	Short Vowel	Long Vowel
can	cane	mad	made
cap	cape	man	mane
dim	dime	mat	mate
fin	fine	rid	ride
mat	mate	rat	rate
pan	pane	van	vane
bit	bite	kit	kite
pin	pine	rip	ripe
cod	code	hop	hope
plan	plane	scrap	scrape
slid	slide	spin	spine
slop	slope	shin	shine

LESSON 11 - WORDS WITH LONG *A* SOUND

Circle the word that matches the picture on the left.

Silent **"e"**

| lake | rake | snake |
| bake | cake | shake |

Silent **"e"**

| age | sage | wage |
| cage | page | stage |

Silent **"e"**

| date | gate | late |
| plate | grate | skate |

Silent **"e"**

| pave | save | wave |
| cave | brave | shave |

| mail | pail | tail |
| rail | fail | snail |

| day | clay | play |
| pray | stay | stray |

Complete the sentence using the correct word.

---

lake   rake   cake   bake   shake

I help my brother _______ the cookies.

---

cage   sage   wage   page   stage

The bird sings and dances in its _______.

---

date   late   mate   grate   skate

We _______ the cheese on top of our pizza.

Complete the sentence using the correct word.

cave   save   wave   brave   shave

The children _________ their hands to say goodbye.

mail   pail   tail   trail   snail

The ________ was very steep and rocky.

day   gray   play   stay   stray

We love to ________ in the park on sunny days.

LESSON 12 - WORDS WITH LONG E SOUND

Circle the word that matches the picture on the left.

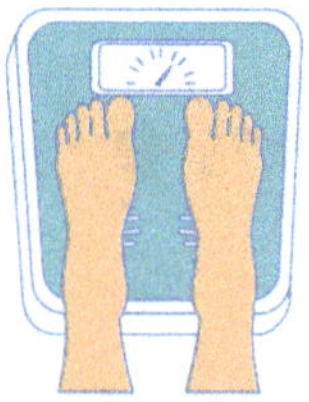	beet	feet	sheet
	deep	sleep	steep
	beam	cream	dream
	team	steam	scream
	fear	hear	clear
	bean	mean	clean
	field	shield	yield
	brief	chief	grief
	beach	peach	teach
	bead	lead	read
	carry	candy	chilly
	honey	money	monkey

Complete the sentence using the correct word.

---

beef   deep   sheep   fleet   sheet

The whales live in the
_______ blue ocean.

---

beam   team   cream   dream   steam

Our _______ won the
game at school.

---

fear   hear   clear   tear   smear

The children ________
the paint on the floor.

LESSON 12 - WORDS WITH LONG E SOUND

Complete the sentence using the correct word.

---

field   yield   shield   brief   grief

Farm animals roam in the open __________.

---

bead   read   beach   peach   teach

Jake builds a sand castle at the __________.

---

honey   money   donkey   monkey

The __________ jumps over the fence.

LESSON 13 - WORDS WITH LONG I SOUND

Circle the word that matches the picture on the left.

Silent **"e"**

lie   tie   pie
hide   ride   slide

Silent **"e"**

dice   mice   rice
twice   price   slice

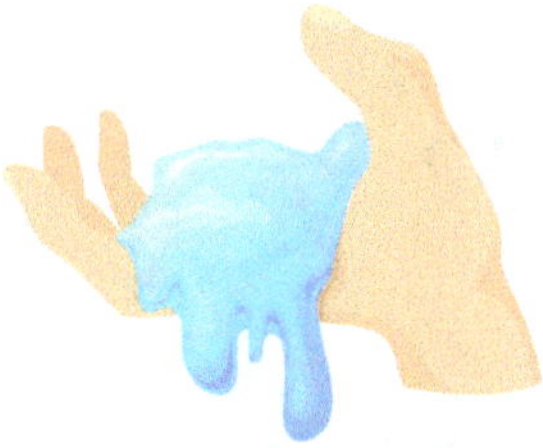

Silent **"e"**

dine   pine   shine
dime   time   slime

Silent **"e"**

bike   hike   like
tile   pile   smile

Silent **"gh"**

high   sigh   thigh
light   night   right

Long i sound of **"y"** and **ye"**

cry   dry   fly
bye   eye   rye

Complete the sentence using the correct word.

---

hide   ride   side   tide   slide

The children enjoyed the train ________ at the park.

---

dice   mice   rice   price   slice

I share a ________ of cake with my mom.

---

dime   time   pine   spine   slime

I drop a ________ into the slot of the piggy bank.

LESSON 13 - WORDS WITH LONG I SOUND

Complete the sentence using the correct word.

bike   hike   pile   tile   smile

Mike and Ike will _______ to the camp.

high   thigh   sigh   tight   right

I look to the left and the _______ before I cross the street.

dry   cry   fly   sky   spy

I will fly my kite when the _______ is clear.

LESSON 14 - WORDS WITH LONG O SOUND

Circle the word that matches the picture on the left.

	cold	hold	scold
	roll	scroll	stroll
"oa"	boat	goat	float
	coast	toast	roast
Silent "e"	joke	poke	smoke
	mole	hole	pole
Silent "e"	bone	cone	stone
	hose	nose	close
Silent "e"	note	vote	wrote
	cove	drove	stove
"ow"	mow	sow	blow
	glow	flow	throw

LESSON 14 - WORDS WITH LONG O SOUND

Complete the sentence using the correct word.

---

cold   **fold**   **sold**   **scold**

My mom _______ a fresh loaf of bread at the market.

---

boat   **coat**   **goat**   **float**

I went fishing with my dad in his tiny _______.

---

joke   **poke**   **broke**   **smoke**

Dark _______ rises from the top of the mountain.

Complete the sentence using the correct word.

roll   toll   scroll   stroll

Kate loves to _______ at the park with her dog.

load   road   toad   board

The _________ to the beach is bumpy.

hole   mole   pole   role

The _________ lives in a hole in the garden.

LESSON 14 - WORDS WITH LONG O SOUND

Complete the sentence using the correct word.

---

bone   cone   stone   phone

Ginger wore a pink _______ hat on her birthday.

---

note   tote   wrote   drove

I _________ a letter to my best friend.

---

glow   blow   flow   throw

I _________ the trash in the garbage bin.

LESSON 15 - WORDS WITH LONG U SOUND

Circle the word that matches the picture on the left.

yoo sound — u, u_e, ue, ew

Silent "e"

| huge | tube | fuse |
| cube | cute | cure |

"u" and "ue"

| mule | mute | music |
| cue | rescue | tissue |

"ew"

| dew | few | new |
| pew | chew | stew |

oo sound — u, ou, oo, ui, ue

|  rude | ruler | ruby |
| tuna | tulip | tunic |

"ou" and "oo"

| soup | group | route |
| hood | good | wood |

"ui" and "ue"

| fruit | suit | juice |
| blue | clue | glue |

Complete the sentence using the correct word.

cute   cube   huge   mule

The ________ carries a heavy load on its back.

cue   hue   tissue   rescue

The boy's ________ from the flood was very scary.

few   new   chew   stew

Mom cooked some meat ________ for lunch.

Complete the sentence using the correct word.

---

rule   rude   ruby   ruler

Kate is now taller than the ______________.

---

tube   tulips   tuna   tunic

I gave my mom a bunch of fresh ______________.

---

soup   group   route   court

A ______________ of students study their lesson.

Complete the sentence using the correct word.

---

dune   duke   tune   June

The camels walk on
the sand _________.

---

fruit   suit   juice   bruise

Mary has a _______ on
her left arm.

---

blue   clue   true   glue

The paw prints gave us a
_______ of what was in
the box.

CONSONANT CLUSTERS (L-BLENDS)
Decoding Words Practice

bl	bl/a/nk	**blank**	bl/e/ss	**bless**
	bl/a/st	**blast**	bl/i/nk	**blink**
	bl/e/nd	**blend**	bl/a/ck	**black**

cl	cl/aw	**claw**	cl/am	**clam**
	cl/ip	**clip**	cl/a/ss	**class**
	cl/og	**clog**	cl/o/ck	**clock**

fl	fl/at	**flat**	fl/e/sh	**flesh**
	fl/ow	**flow**	fl/a/sh	**flash**
	fl/ip	**flip**	fl/ow/er	**flower**

gl	gl/ad	**glad**	gl/a/ss	**glass**
	gl/ow	**glow**	gl/o/be	**globe**
	gl/ea/m	**gleam**	gl/a/re	**glare**

pl	pl/a/nt	**plant**	pl/a/te	**plate**
	pl/um	**plum**	pl/a/ne	**plane**
	pl/u/ck	**pluck**	pl/an/et	**planet**

sl	sl/am	**slam**	sl/a/nt	**slant**
	sl/ed	**sled**	sl/ee/p	**sleep**
	sl/ug	**slug**	sl/ur/p	**slurp**

CONSONANT CLUSTERS (R-BLENDS)

Decoding Words Practice

br	br/i/ng	**bring**	br/ea/d	**bread**
	br/i/sk	**brisk**	br/ow/n	**brown**
	br/ai/n	**brain**	br/oo/m	**broom**
cr	cr/ab	**crab**	cr/a/ck	**crack**
	cr/a/ft	**craft**	cr/u/mb	**crumb**
	cr/o/ss	**cross**	cr/ea/m	**cream**
dr	dr/ag	**drag**	dr/i/ft	**drift**
	dr/aw	**draw**	dr/i/nk	**drink**
	dr/op	**drop**	dr/ea/m	**dream**
fr	fr/og	**frog**	fr/o/nt	**front**
	fr/e/sh	**fresh**	fr/ie/nd	**friend**
	fr/ui/t	**fruit**	fr/ee/ze	**freeze**
gr	gr/ab	**grab**	gr/ee/n	**green**
	gr/ay	**gray**	gr/ow/l	**growl**
	gr/a/ss	**grass**	gr/ee/t	**greet**
pr	pr/i/nt	**print**	pr/ay	**pray**
	pr/i/ze	**prize**	pr/ai/se	**praise**
	pr/e/ss	**press**	pr/in/ce	**prince**
tr	tr/ap	**trap**	tr/u/ck	**truck**
	tr/im	**trim**	tr/ai/n	**train**
	tr/ip	**trip**	tr/u/st	**trust**

CONSONANT CLUSTERS (S-BLENDS)
Decoding Words Practice

sc	sc/an	**scan**		sc/o/re	**score**
	sc/a/lp	**scalp**		sc/a/le	**scale**
	sc/ar/f	**scarf**		sc/oo/p	**scoop**
sk	sk/in	**skin**		sk/ir/t	**skirt**
	sk/im	**skim**		sk/u/ll	**skull**
	sk/ip	**skip**		sk/u/nk	**skunk**
sm	sm/a/ll	**small**		sm/ea/r	**smear**
	sm/ar/t	**smart**		sm/a/sh	**smash**
	sm/o/g	**smog**		sm/oo/th	**smooth**
sn	sn/ap	**snap**		sn/o/re	**snore**
	sn/ag	**snag**		sn/ou/t	**snout**
	sn/a/ck	**snack**		sn/ee/ze	**sneeze**
sp	sp/in	**spin**		sp/e/ck	**speck**
	sp/an	**span**		sp/e/nd	**spend**
	sp/a/rk	**spark**		sp/ee/d	**speed**
st	st/ep	**step**		st/a/ck	**stack**
	st/op	**stop**		st/or/m	**storm**
	st/a/nd	**stand**		st/it/ch	**stitch**
sw	sw/ap	**swap**		sw/it/ch	**switch**
	sw/ing	**swing**		sw/ee/t	**sweet**
	sw/ee/p	**sweep**		sw/oo/p	**swoop**

CONSONANT CLUSTERS

Decoding Words Practice

scr	scr/ap scr/ew	**scrap** **screw**	scr/i/pt scr/ea/m	**script** **scream**
squ	squ/at squ/in/t	**squat** **squint**	squ/a/sh squ/ir/m	**squash** **squirm**
str	str/ap str/aw	**strap** **straw**	str/a/nd str/u/ck	**strand** **struck**
spr	spr/ing spr/aw/l	**spring** **sprawl**	spr/ou/t spr/ea/d	**sprout** **spread**
spl	spl/it spl/a/sh	**split** **splash**	spl/i/nt spl/i/ce	**splint** **splice**
thr	thr/oa/t thr/a/sh	**throat** **thrash**	thr/ea/d thr/ow	**thread** **throw**
tw	tw/in tw/ee/t	**twin** **tweet**	tw/i/st tw/ir/l	**twist** **twirl**
qu	qu/ar/t qu/e/st	**quart** **quest**	qu/i/lt qu/en/ch	**quilt** **quench**

ENDING CONSONANT CLUSTERS

Decoding Words Practice.

ct	a/ct	**act**	t/a/ct	**tact**
	f/a/ct	**fact**	d/u/ct	**duct**
ft	g/i/ft	**gift**	s/o/ft	**soft**
	l/e/ft	**left**	l/o/ft	**loft**
ld	c/o/ld	**cold**	f/o/ld	**fold**
	g/o/ld	**gold**	m/o/ld	**mold**
lp	h/e/lp	**help**	k/e/lp	**kelp**
	g/u/lp	**gulp**	p/u/lp	**pulp**
lt	m/e/lt	**melt**	b/o/lt	**bolt**
	f/au/lt	**fault**	j/o/lt	**jolt**
mp	c/a/mp	**camp**	b/u/mp	**bump**
	ch/a/mp	**champ**	st/u/mp	**stump**
nd	l/a/nd	**land**	br/a/nd	**brand**
	p/o/nd	**pond**	st/a/nd	**stand**
nk	r/a/nk	**rank**	pl/u/nk	**plunk**
	t/a/nk	**tank**	sk/u/nk	**skunk**

ENDING CONSONANT CLUSTERS
Decoding Words Practice

nt	t/e/nt	**tent**	r/e/nt	**rent**
	h/i/nt	**hint**	f/ai/nt	**faint**
pt	k/e/pt	**kept**	cr/e/pt	**crept**
	sl/e/pt	**slept**	w/e/pt	**wept**
rd	h/a/rd	**hard**	w/o/rd	**word**
	b/oa/rd	**board**	h/ea/rd	**heard**
rk	d/a/rk	**dark**	w/o/rk	**work**
	cl/e/rk	**clerk**	st/o/rk	**stork**
sk	w/i/sk	**wisk**	d/u/sk	**dusk**
	t/a/sk	**task**	fl/a/sk	**flask**
sp	g/a/sp	**gasp**	cl/a/sp	**clasp**
	w/a/sp	**wasp**	gr/a/sp	**grasp**
st	b/e/st	**best**	fr/o/st	**frost**
	ch/e/st	**chest**	r/oa/st	**roast**

CONSONANT DIGRAPH

Decoding Words Practice

sh	sh/in	**shin**	sh/oe	**shoe**
	sh/ip	**ship**	sh/ar/k	**shark**
	sh/op	**shop**	sh/a/ke	**shake**
sh (ending sound)	c/a/sh	**cash**	b/u/sh	**bush**
	d/a/sh	**dash**	w/i/sh	**wish**
	f/i/sh	**fish**	sm/a/sh	**smash**
ch	ch/in	**chin**	ch/a/nt	**chant**
	ch/ip	**chip**	ch/u/nk	**chunk**
	ch/op	**chop**	ch/ur/ch	**church**
ch (ending sound)	b/en/ch	**bench**	p/in/ch	**pinch**
	b/un/ch	**bunch**	p/er/ch	**perch**
	l/un/ch	**lunch**	wr/en/ch	**wrench**
th (soft sound)	th/in	**thin**	th/a/nk	**thank**
	th/ud	**thud**	th/i/nk	**think**
	th/i/ck	**thick**	th/u/mb	**thumb**
th (ending soft sound)	b/a/th	**bath**	cl/o/th	**cloth**
	p/a/th	**path**	br/o/th	**broth**
	m/a/th	**math**	ea/r/th	**earth**

CONSONANT DIGRAPH

Decoding Words Practice

th (hard sound)	th/is	**this**	th/at	**that**
	th/em	**them**	th/ey	**they**
	th/an	**than**	th/en	**then**
wh	wh/at	**what**	wh/a/le	**whale**
	wh/en	**when**	wh/ee/l	**wheel**
	wh/i/ch	**which**	wh/i/sk	**whisk**
ph	ph/o/ne	**phone**	ph/a/se	**phase**
	ph/o/to	**photo**	phr/a/se	**phrase**
ng	s/i/ng	**sing**	s/o/ng	**song**
	w/i/ng	**wing**	str/o/ng	**strong**
	br/i/ng	**bring**	str/i/ng	**string**
gh	c/ou/gh	**cough**	t/ou/gh	**tough**
	r/ou/gh	**rough**	l/au/gh	**laugh**

VOWEL DIGRAPHS/DIPHTHONGS

Decoding Words Practice

ai long a sound	r/ai/n ch/ai/n pl/ai/n	**rain** **chain** **plain**	st/ai/n br/ai/n gr/ai/n	**stain** **brain** **grain**
ea long e sound	ea/t m/ea/t tr/ea/t	**eat** **meat** **treat**	fl/ea b/ea/ch l/ea/sh	**flea** **beach** **leash**
ea short e sound	h/ea/d br/ea/d thr/ea/d	**head** **bread** **thread**	d/ea/d dr/ea/d spr/ea/d	**dead** **dread** **spread**
ea long a sound	b/ea/r p/ea/r t/ea/r	**bear** **pear** **tear**	br/ea/k st/ea/k gr/ea/t	**break** **steak** **great**
ee long e sound	b/ee/t sw/ee/t str/ee/t	**beet** **sweet** **street**	j/ee/p k/ee/p sw/ee/p	**jeep** **keep** **sweep**
ey long e sound	a/ll/ey h/on/ey m/on/ey	**alley** **honey** **money**	t/ur/k/ey ch/im/n/ey p/ar/sl/ey	**turkey** **chimney** **parsley**

VOWEL DIGRAPHS/DIPHTHONGS

Decoding Words Practice

oa long o sound	b/oa/t	**boat**	t/oa/st	**toast**
	g/oa/t	**goat**	r/oa/st	**roast**
	fl/oa/t	**float**	thr/oa/t	**throat**
ow	cr/ow	**crow**	fl/ow	**flow**
	sh/ow	**show**	gl/ow	**glow**
	sn/ow	**snow**	sl/ow	**slow**
oy	b/oy	**boy**	s/oy	**soy**
	j/oy	**joy**	pl/oy	**ploy**
	t/oy	**toy**	en/j/oy	**enjoy**
au	h/au/l	**haul**	au/nt	**aunt**
	h/au/nt	**haunt**	f/au/lt	**fault**
	t/au/nt	**taunt**	v/au/lt	**vault**
aw	r/aw	**raw**	f/aw/n	**fawn**
	p/aw	**paw**	h/aw/k	**hawk**
	cl/aw	**claw**	str/aw	**straw**

VOWEL DIGRAPHS/DIPHTHONGS

Decoding Words Practice

ei long a sound	v/ei/n	**vein**	b/ei/ge	**beige**
	v/ei/l	**veil**	w/ei/gh	**weigh**
ie long e sound	n/ie/ce	**niece**	ch/ie/f	**chief**
	f/ie/ld	**field**	th/ie/f	**thief**
	sh/ie/ld	**shield**	gr/ie/f	**grief**
ay long a sound	h/ay	**hay**	cl/ay	**clay**
	pl/ay	**play**	tr/ay	**tray**
	spr/ay	**spray**	st/ay	**stay**
ui long u sound "oo"	s/ui/t	**suit**	j/ui/ce	**juice**
	fr/ui/t	**fruit**	br/ui/se	**bruise**
ui short i sound	b/ui/ld	**build**	g/ui/ld	**guild**
	g/ui/lt	**guilt**	g/ui/t/ar	**guitar**

VOWEL DIGRAPHS/DIPHTHONGS

Decoding Words Practice

oe long o sound "oo"	d/oe	**doe**	h/oe	**hoe**
	t/oe	**toe**	al/oe	**aloe**
ue long u sound "oo"	cl/ue	**clue**	bl/ue	**blue**
	tr/ue	**true**	gl/ue	**glue**
ue long u sound "yoo"	d/ue	**due**	v/en/ue	**venue**
	c/ue	**cue**	ar/g/ue	**argue**
ew long u sound "yoo"	d/ew	**dew**	ch/ew	**chew**
	p/ew	**pew**	st/ew	**stew**
	n/ew	**new**	sk/ew	**skew**
oo long "o" sound	m/oo/n	**moon**	sm/oo/th	**smooth**
	n/oo/n	**noon**	g/oo/se	**goose**
	sp/oo/n	**spoon**	m/oo/se	**moose**
oo short sound	h/oo/k	**hook**	b/oo/k	**book**
	n/oo/k	**nook**	g/oo/d	**good**
	l/oo/k	**look**	w/oo/d	**wood**

VOWEL DIGRAPHS/DIPHTHONGS

Decoding Words Practice

oi "oy"	c/oi/l	**coil**	b/oi/l	**boil**
	c/oi/n	**coin**	br/oi/l	**broil**
	f/oi/l	**foil**	sp/oi/l	**spoil**
ou "ow"	fl/ou/r	**flour**	cl/ou/d	**cloud**
	s/ou/r	**sour**	h/ou/se	**house**
	s/ou/nd	**sound**	m/ou/th	**mouth**
ou short o sound "uh"	t/ou/gh	**tough**	y/ou/ng	**young**
	r/ou/gh	**rough**	d/ou/ble	**double**
	t/ou/ch	**touch**	c/ou/ple	**couple**
ou long u sound "oo"	t/ou/r	**tour**	c/ou/rt	**court**
	p/ou/r	**pour**	r/ou/te	**route**
ou long o sound	y/ou	**you**	s/ou/p	**soup**
	y/ou/th	**youth**	gr/ou/p	**group**
ou sound as in "wood"	silent "l" c/ou/ld	**could**	sh/ou/ld	**should**
	w/ou/ld	**would**		

ANSWER KEY

Lesson 2 - Short Vowel and Consonant Blends

Page 11	**Page 13**	**Page 15**
yam	mad	nap
fan	dad	mat
ram	wag	cap
jam	sad	map
pan	bag	car
can	pad	jar
ham	tag	bat
van	rag	fat

Page 17	**Page 19**	**Page 21**
leg	pen	big
red	den	bin
wed	vet	win
keg	wet	fig
beg	men	fin
fed	hen	pin
bed	jet	dip
	pet	sip

Page 23	**Page 25**	**Page 27**
pot	mug	bun
log	bug	fun
dog	tub	nut
pop	cub	run
mop	tug	hut
hot	rub	sun
top	hug	cut
hop		

ANSWER KEY

Lesson 3 - Consonant Clusters（L Blends）

Page 35	**Page 40**	**Page 41**	**Page 42**
blue	blow	flag	play
class	blocks	flock	plate
	bloom	floor	plums
Page 37			
flips	______	______	______
gloves	clown	glide	sleep
	climb	glue	slide
Page 39	clouds	glass	slow
plane			
sloth			

Lesson 4 - Consonant Clusters（R Blends）

Page 46	**Page 52**	**Page 53**	**Page 54**
braid	brown	frog	growl
crawls	brush	fruits	grill
	bricks	friend	green
Page 48			
dream	______	______	______
free	crab	drums	prince
	crunchy	draw	pray
Page 50	crack	dress	pretty
grow			
press			
Page 51			
treats			

ANSWER KEY

Lesson 5 - Consonant Clusters (S Blends)

Page 58	**Page 64**	**Page 65**	**Page 66**	**Page 67**
scout	scarf	smell	spot	slope
skip	score	smile	spin	slam
	scare	small	spark	sled

Page 60				
smart				
snail	skunk	snow	stack	swim
	ski	sniff	stop	sweeps
	skirt	snake	sticks	swing

Page 62

speak

step

Page 63

swan

Lesson 6 - Other Consonant Clusters

Page 71	**Page 73**	**Page 75**
scrubs	stream	splash
squeak	spread	throne
		twinkle

Lesson 7 - Ending Consonant Clusters

Page 79	**Page 81**	**Page 83**	**Page 85**
act	fold	belt	pond
sift	help	pump	tank

Page 89	**Page 91**	**Page 93**
count	third	flask
sculpt	bark	wasp
		roast

ANSWER KEY

Lesson 8 - Consonant Digraph

Page 97

ship
trash

Page 99

cheese
lunch

Page 101

thick
bath

Page 103

They
whale

Page 105

photo
sling
laugh

Lesson 9 - Double Consonants

Page 110

guess
pillow
glitter

Page 111

cotton
puffy
chubby

Page 112

hidden
happy
juggle

Page 113

summer
furry
buzzer

Lesson 11 - Words with long a sound

Page 122

cake   snail
cage   play
grate

Page 123

rake
cage
grate

Page 124

wave
trail
play

Lesson 12 - Words with long e sound

Page 125

feet   chief
dream   teach
hear   honey

Page 126

deep
team
smear

Page 127

field
beach
donkey

ANSWER KEY

Lesson 13 - Words with long i sound

Page 128

hide	light
slice	fly
hike	

Page 129

ride
slice
dime

Page 130

hike
right
sky

Lesson 14 - Words with long o sound

Page 131

stroll	hose
float	stove
hole	mow

Page 132

sold
boat
smoke

Page 133

stroll
road
mole

Page 134

cone
wrote
throw

Lesson 15 - Words with long u sound

Page 135

cube	tulip
music	soup
chew	clue

Page 136

mule
rescue
stew

Page 137

ruler
tulips
group

Page 138

dune
bruise
clue